STUDY GUIDE

Discover JUDGES

by
Marilyn A. McGinnis

Grand Rapids, Michigan

Unless otherwise noted, Scripture quotations in this publication are from the Holy Bible, Today's New International Version (TNIV), © 2001, 2005 by International Bible Society. All rights reserved worldwide.

Cover photo: iStock

Discover Your Bible series. *Discover Judges* (Study Guide), © 2009 by Faith Alive Christian Resources, 2850 Kalamazoo Ave. SE, Grand Rapids, MI 49560. All rights reserved. With the exception of brief excerpts for review purposes, no part of this book may be reproduced in any manner whatsoever without written permission from the publisher. Printed in the United States of America.

We welcome your comments. Call us at 1-800-333-8300 or e-mail us at editors@faithaliveresources.org.

ISBN 978-1-59255-481-2

5 4 3 2 1

Contents

How to Study 4

Introduction 5

Map: Land of the Twelve Tribes 6

Glossary of Terms 7

Lesson 1
    A Time of Testing 10

Lesson 2
    The First Judges—Othniel Through Deborah 13

Lesson 3
    Gideon—Trust, Triumph, and Then 17

Lesson 4
    Abimelek—the Man Who Would Be King 22

Lesson 5
    Jephthah—from Outcast to Warrior-Leader 26

Lesson 6
    Samson—Used by God in Spite of Himself 30

Lesson 7
    Samson and Delilah—From Revenge to Ruin 34

Lesson 8
    Rock Bottom of Moral Decay 38

Lesson 9
    A People Divided and Still Sustained 42

An Invitation and Prayer of Commitment 45

Bibliography 46

Evaluation Questionnaire

How to Study

The questions in this study booklet will help you discover for yourself what the Bible says. This is inductive Bible study—in which you will discover the message for yourself.

Questions are the key to inductive Bible study. Through questions you search for the writers' thoughts and ideas. The questions in this booklet are designed to help you in your quest for answers. You can and should ask your own questions too. The Bible comes alive with meaning for many people as they discover the exciting truths it contains. Our hope and prayer is that this booklet will help the Bible come alive for you.

The questions in this study are designed to be used with Today's New International Version of the Bible, but other translations can also be used.

Step 1. Read each Bible passage several times. Allow the ideas to sink in. Think about their meaning. Ask questions about the passage.

Step 2. Answer the questions, drawing your answers from the passage. Remember that the purpose of the study is to discover what the Bible says. Write your answers in your own words. If you use Bible study aids such as commentaries or Bible handbooks, do so only after completing your own personal study.

Step 3. Apply the Bible's message to your own life. Ask,

- What is this passage saying to me?
- How does it challenge me? Comfort me? Encourage me?
- Is there a promise I should claim? A warning I should heed?
- For what can I give thanks?

If you sense God speaking to you in some way, respond to God in a personal prayer.

Step 4. Share your thoughts with someone else if possible. This will be easiest if you are part of a Bible study group that meets regularly to share discoveries and discuss questions.

If you would like to learn of a study group in your area or would like information on training to start a small group Bible study,

- call toll-free 1-888-644-0814, e-mail smallgroups@crcna.org, or visit www.smallgroupministries.org

- call toll-free 1-800-333-8300 or visit www.FaithAliveResources.org (to order materials)

Introduction

The book of Judges picks up the story of Israel where the book of Joshua left off. Joshua became the people's leader after Moses had died (Josh. 1:1-6), and in obedience to God Joshua led the people into the promised land. At the Lord's leading, they fought many battles and captured many cities, and each of the twelve tribes of Israel was now assigned an inheritance of land. Though many of the Canaanites were conquered, some still remained, so there was still work to be done.

Joshua promised the people, "The LORD . . . will push [the Canaanites] out for your sake. He will drive them out before you, and you will take possession of their land, as . . . God promised" (Josh. 23:5). God had first made this promise to Abraham about 700 years earlier, saying that his descendants (Israel) would receive the land from God when the sin of the peoples living there had reached "its full measure" (Gen. 15:16-20).

Joshua also reminded the people that they had made promises to God. Israel had promised not to worship the gods of the Canaanites or mix with the foreign powers around them. "The LORD has driven out before you great and powerful nations," Joshua said, "but if you turn away and ally yourselves with . . . these nations . . . the LORD your God will no longer drive out these nations before you" (Josh. 23:9, 12-13).

Near the end of his life Joshua challenged the people, saying, "Choose for yourselves this day whom you will serve," and he set this example for them: "As for me and my household, we will serve the LORD." And the people said, "We too will serve the LORD" (Josh. 24:15, 18).

But did the people mean what they said? Or was this a fair-weather response during a time of peace?

The book of Judges records a period of about 300 years between the death of Joshua and the beginning of the monarchy (era of kings) in Israel. During this time God appointed judges to rule over the people and to lead them through times when they needed deliverance from enemies.

The main theme of Judges is that God is faithful despite the unfaithfulness of his people. Though some of the stories in Judges pose shocking twists and puzzling turns, we discover that human nature isn't much different than it was a few thousand years ago. As a result, this study will often challenge us with issues that apply to our lives today.

God bless you as you study this book of the Bible together.

Note: Because of the narrative (storytelling) nature of this book, some accounts covered in the lessons of this study are lengthy, spanning two or more chapters of Scripture. This may call for more reading than your group is used to, so you may wish to read ahead in your Bibles at home before doing some of the lessons together.

Land of the Twelve Tribes

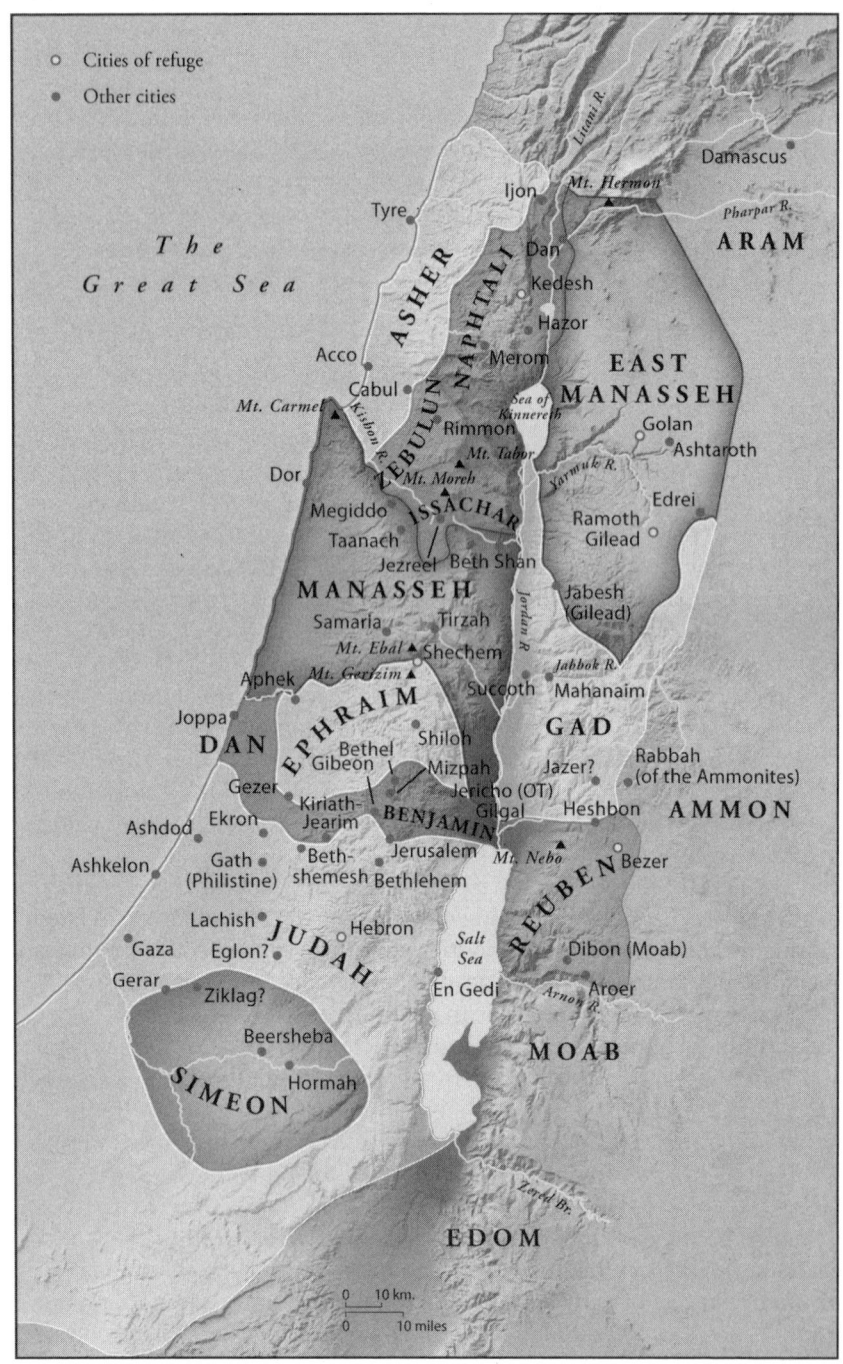

—used by permission of Zondervan Corporation. All rights reserved.

Glossary of Terms

altar—a stone or heap of stones on which people laid animals or grain as sacrifices.

Amalekites—descendants of Esau (Gen. 36:12, 16).

Ammonites— descendants of Lot through his younger daughter (Gen. 19:36-38).

angel of the Lord—This figure appears at times to God's people (often as a man) and makes announcements or judgments in God's name (see Gen. 16:7; 22:11-18; Josh. 5:13-15; Judg. 6:11-12; 13:2-23). Sometimes this angel is also referred to as "the LORD" (for example, see Gen. 16:13; Judg. 6:14), and the *TNIV Study Bible* explains that "as the LORD's personal messenger who represented him and bore his credentials, the angel could speak on behalf of (and so be identified with) the One who sent him." (See also Ex. 23:20-23; Josh. 5:13-15.)

ark of the covenant—a wooden chest overlaid with gold that was placed in the innermost room (Most Holy Place) of the tabernacle (tent of meeting) or, later, in the temple (1 Kings 8). It symbolized the presence of God among his people (see Ex. 25:10-22). In Judges 20:27 we learn that sometimes the ark was moved to other places, even though the tabernacle was set up in a designated town (Shiloh—see 18:31).

Bethel—Bethel means "house of God" and is a significant location in Bible history. Abraham built an altar there after entering the promised land (Gen. 12:7-8; 13:3-4). Jacob had a vision of God at Bethel (Gen. 28:10-19). In Judges 20:27 we find that the ark of the covenant was temporarily at Bethel, with Phinehas the priest "ministering before it."

Baal and Ashtoreth (Asherah)—Canaanite god and goddess of fertility and war.

burnt offering—a sacrifice laid on an altar and completely burned.

Canaanites—occupants of the promised land of Canaan. This land was named after a grandson of Noah (Gen. 9:18). The peoples who lived in Canaan before Israel came had various tribal or regional names (such as Hittites, Amorites, Midianites, Perizzites, Hivites, Jebusites, Philistines, and Sidonians) and were also generally called Canaanites.

clean—God allowed people to eat certain kinds of animals and to use them for sacrifices. These were referred to as "clean"; all other animals were considered "unclean" (see Lev. 11).

concubine—a secondary wife who might also be a slave.

covenant—a mutually binding agreement between two parties; usually both parties agree to accept certain responsibilities.

ephah—a measure equaling about three-fifths of a bushel (22 liters).

ephod—a special garment worn by the high priest (Ex. 28:6-14). It could also refer to an object associated with idol worship (Judg. 17:5; 18:14).

Gibeah—a city within the tribe of Benjamin where the gang rape of a concubine took place. It and its inhabitants were destroyed by the rest of the tribes of Israel.

Israel—see **twelve tribes of Israel**.

judges—men or women chosen to arbitrate judicial matters, but also to lead the Israelites in battle against the Canaanites and other foreign powers.

lot casting—Casting lots or drawing lots can be done in many ways—by flipping a coin, throwing dice or other small objects with marks on them, drawing sticks of different lengths, pulling marked or different-colored pieces out of a hat, and so on. The lots approved by God for use in Israel were the Urim and Thummim, to be placed in the breastpiece of the sacred ephod worn by the priest of God (Ex. 28:30). See Numbers 27:18-21 for the Lord's instructions on lot casting in Joshua's day. Note as well that the land divisions in Canaan were determined by lot (Num. 26:55-56; 33:54; 34:13-17).

Midianites— descendants of Abraham's son Midian through his second wife, Keturah (Gen. 25:1-2).

Moabites—descendants of Lot through his older daughter (Gen. 19:36-38).

Molek—a god worshiped by the Canaanites; sometimes this worship involved the sacrifice of children by fire.

Moses—the leader of the Israelites when God delivered them from slavery in Egypt and as they lived in the wilderness before entering the promised land (Palestine). Moses received the law from God and taught it to the Israelites.

Nazirite—a person who took a vow to be set apart to God. The vow included restrictions such as not drinking wine and not cutting one's hair and could be temporary or long-term. Samson was dedicated to be a Nazirite from birth and throughout his whole life (Judg. 13:2-7; see also 1 Sam. 1:10-11; Luke 1:11-17).

oath—a binding promise that often involved swearing by something or someone greater than oneself.

ox goad—a long stick with a sharp point for prodding oxen.

Perizzites—a people who lived in Canaan from before the time of Abraham (Gen. 13:7). Their origin is obscure and unknown.

Philistines—descendants of a grandson of Noah's son Ham who, in the time of the judges, occupied a strip of land along the Mediterranean Sea from Gaza to Egypt.

prophecy—a message from someone who speaks God's Word to the people. The person who spoke a prophecy was a prophet.

sacrifice—the act of offering something precious to God. Unbelievers also made sacrifices to false gods. In the Old Testament this was usually an animal (the best of the flock) or the firstfruits of a harvest.

Shechem—a town known as the place where Abraham built an altar to God when he first arrived in Canaan. It was one of the six cities of refuge set up by Joshua, and the place where he delivered his farewell address. In the time of the judges it was a center of pagan Canaanite worship.

shekel—a unit of weight used to weigh silver and gold. In the time of the judges, ten shekels of silver was considered a decent yearly wage (Judg. 17:10).

sign—a miraculous event sought by Gideon to confirm that he should do what God told him to do.

sin—going against God's will; disobeying God's commands.

Spirit of the Lord—In the Old Testament the Holy Spirit came upon certain individuals to empower them to accomplish certain things.

threshing—In ancient times, farmers usually threshed their grain in an open area by having cattle walk on it to loosen the grain from the stalks or by drawing toothed sledges through it. In Judges 6 we read of Gideon threshing his grain in a winepress to keep the Midianites from stealing or destroying it.

twelve tribes of Israel—Jacob (whose name was changed by God to Israel) had twelve sons: Reuben, Simeon, Levi, Judah, Zebulun, Issachar, Dan, Gad, Asher, Naphtali, Joseph, and Benjamin (Gen. 49). Joseph's two sons, Ephraim and Manasseh, are half-tribes but are sometimes referred to as separate tribes, making it appear (erroneously) as though there were thirteen tribes in all.

worship—reverence and respect given to God; acknowledging God's worthiness to be praised and served.

Lesson 1
Judges 1:1-3:6

A Time of Testing

Introductory Notes

In the opening chapters of Judges we can glimpse the general situation in Israel "after the death of Joshua" (Judg. 1:1), by whom God brought the people into the promised land of Canaan. Though the Israelites had mainly overtaken the land by this time, they had to continue battling the Canaanites, who were often powerful enemies. The Israelites had to rout these peoples because God said their wickedness had "reached its full measure" (see Gen. 15:16), and the Canaanites' punishment included losing their land to make way for God's people to live there.

This period became a time of testing for Israel. Let's see how the people responded to God in this era of their history.

1. *Judges 1:1-20*

    a. How do the people begin their task of routing the Canaanites who remained in the land?

    b. What do these first twenty verses show us about God's support of his people? What does it mean when the people begin to fail?

2. **Judges 1:21-36**
   a. Describe the successes and/or failures of the Israelite tribes mentioned in these verses. List the tribes, if you like, and assign each one a success rate.

   b. What pattern do you see emerging here?

3. **Judges 2:1-5**
   a. What does God announce through the angel of the Lord?

   b. How should we interpret the people's sorrow?

4. **Judges 2:6-3:6**
   a. Judges 2:6-9 mentions the death of Joshua again (see Judges 1:1). Compare this with Joshua 24:28-30.

b. Describe how far the people fell away from the Lord after the generation under Joshua's leadership died.

c. How did the Lord respond to the people's disobedience and then to their cries of distress?

d. What did the Lord conclude because of the people's longlasting disobedience and stubbornness?

e. What would be the significance of teaching warfare to later generations of Israel?

Questions for Reflection

What characteristics of God have you (re)discovered in the Scriptures for this lesson? How does God demonstrate these characteristics?

Why was the Israelites' obedience to God so important? What were the results if they obeyed? If they did not obey? Why do we sometimes find it hard to obey God?

Lesson 2
Judges 3:7-5:31

The First Judges—Othniel Through Deborah

Introductory Notes

After explaining the Israelites' failed attempts to conquer the Canaanites, the writer now introduces several people God appointed as judges. As we have noted, the period of the judges began soon after the death of Joshua and ended when the monarchy in Israel began (see 1 Sam. 8).

Some of the judges may be well known to us. But others are mentioned only briefly and may not be familiar to us at all. Yet their stories are included for a reason. The chronicle of their times helps us recognize the futility of life lived in disobedience. That's the bad news. But there is also good news as we discover that the Spirit of God is actively involved, even in this delinquent period of Israel's history. No way has God forgotten his people.

1. *Judges 3:7-11*
   a. What does it mean to do "evil in the eyes of the LORD"?

   b. What is God's response to the Israelites' evil ways?

   c. By what power is Othniel able to deliver the Israelites?

2. *Judges 3:12-31*
   a. What makes it possible for Eglon king of Moab to subdue the Israelites?

   b. What do we learn about Ehud, and how does he help to deliver Israel?

   c. What does the brief account of Israel's next deliverer tell us?

3. *Judges 4:1-3*
   Note the continuing cycle of disobedience. What do the Israelites do? How long and by what means does God punish them this time?

4. *Judges 4:4-16*
   a. What do we learn about Deborah in these verses? About Barak?

b. Why do you think Barak refuses to go into battle without Deborah? What does Deborah say about that?

c. Notice the positions of the armies. Where are Sisera and his men and chariots? Where are Barak and Deborah and their army? Which army has the advantage? Why?

d. Describe the outcome of the battle.

5. *Judges 4:17-24*
Who is Jael, and how does she deal with Sisera?

6. *Judges 5*
   a. The Song of Deborah is sung by both Deborah and Barak after Sisera and his army have been destroyed. How would you describe this song?

15

b. What was life like in Israel when God called Deborah to lead the people? (See Judg. 5:6-9.) Did this mean all was lost? Explain.

c. After describing the heroism of Jael, this song focuses on another woman, Sisera's mother (Judg. 5:28-30). What do we learn from this section of the song?

d. How does the song end?

Questions for Reflection

In what ways can you identify with Deborah in this story? With Barak? Jael? Is there a way you might also relate to other characters? Explain.

As you reflect on the various characters in this story, consider each one's relationship with God—or lack thereof. Then give yourself a few minutes to reflect quietly on your own relationship with God. Where is God in your life at this point in time?

Lesson 3
Judges 6-8

Gideon—Trust, Triumph, and Then . . .

Introductory Notes

After the land has had peace for forty years, the Israelites again do "evil in the eyes of the LORD" (Judg. 5:31-6:1). Despite the victory of Deborah and Barak over the local Canaanites, the Israelites haven't changed much, if at all. Enter the Midianites who, along with some of their allies, begin to torment the Israelites unmercifully. Let's see what God in his mercy does next for his people.

1. *Judges 6:1-10*
   Briefly describe the situation in Israel as told in these verses.

2. *Judges 6:11-24*
   a. How does the angel of the Lord encourage and challenge Gideon? Why?

   b. How would you describe Gideon and his reactions in this scene?

3. *Judges 6:25-32*
   a. What does God tell Gideon to do next, and why would God command this?

   b. How does Gideon carry out God's command, and how do people react to this?

4. *Judges 6:33-40*
   a. As Gideon calls on people from Israel to fight with him against Midian, what does he ask of the Lord, and how does God respond?

   b. What does this reveal to us about Gideon and about God?

5. *Judges 7:1-8*
   How does God reduce the number of soldiers in Gideon's army? Why does God do this?

6. *Judges 7:9-18*
   a. What does God do next to encourage Gideon and his army?

   b. How does Gideon respond?

7. *Judges 7:19-25*
   a. Describe Gideon's instructions and the unusual way in which this battle will begin.

   b. How does the Lord bring victory for Israel through Gideon's leadership?

8. *Judges 8:1-21*
   a. Though the Ephraimites have helped by capturing two Midianite leaders, they present Gideon with a challenge. Why? How does Gideon handle this situation?

b. Mop-up operations are hampered by uncooperative people in Sukkoth and Peniel as well. What happens in those towns, and how does Gideon handle the people's disrespect?

c. How does Gideon capture the kings of Midian, and what does he do with them?

9. *Judges 8:22-27*
   What kind of leadership does Gideon give Israel when they ask him to rule over them?

10. *Judges 8:28-33*
    How would you describe Gideon's later years?

Questions for Reflection

What have we learned about Gideon in this lesson? What have we learned about God?

How would you describe the life of Gideon to someone who hasn't heard it before?

Though the account of Gideon and the Midianites is one of the great deliverance stories of God's people, we can see that this summary statement of Judges aptly describes the life and times of Gideon: "In those days Israel had no king; everyone did as they saw fit" (Judg. 17:6; 21:25). Reflect individually or together on whether this statement describes our own life and times.

Though we can always depend on God to be faithful, are there any areas in our lives in which we are not faithful to God? If so, what can we do about serving God more faithfully?

Lesson 4
Judges 9:1-10:5

Abimelek—the Man Who Would Be King

Introductory Notes

After Gideon's death, his son Abimelek decides that he should be king over Israel. But Gideon had said, "I will not rule over you, nor will my son rule over you. The LORD will rule over you" (Judg. 8:23). Though Gideon was not faithful to God later in life, he did speak wisely here.

Many years earlier Moses had said to the people, "When you enter the land the LORD your God is giving you and have taken possession of it and settled in it, and you say, 'Let us set a king over us like all the nations around us,' be sure to appoint over you the king the LORD your God chooses" (Deut. 17:14-15).

Let's see what happens as Abimelek aims to be king.

1. *Judges 9:1-6*

   a. How does Abimelek round up support for his desire to be king?

   b. How does he clear away opposition to his kingship?

   c. Gideon said that neither he nor his son would rule over the people (8:23). Besides that, the land was at peace. So why does Abimelek raise the question of who will rule over Israel?

2. *Judges 9:7-21*
   a. How does Jotham challenge the people of Shechem to act honorably and wisely?

   b. What are the main points of the story Jotham tells?

3. *Judges 9:22-29*
   a. How does conflict develop between Abimelek and the people of Shechem?

   b. What happens when Gaal son of Ebed moves into town?

4. *Judges 9:30-49*
   a. Some people in Shechem are still loyal to Abimelek. Who are they, and how do they help Abimelek?

    b. Describe how Abimelek sets up his attacks on Gaal and on the people of Shechem.

    c. What is ironic about these attacks?

5. *Judges 9:50-57*
    a. How do Abimelek's days come to an end?

    b. How does the writer of Judges explain the outcome of Abimelek's life?

6. *Judges 10:1-5*
What do we learn about the judges Tola and Jair?

Questions for Reflection
>What have you learned about the art of storytelling in this Scripture passage? (Consider the uses of irony, parallelism, telling a story within a story, providing narration to explain and summarize, and so on.)
>
>How would you present this story to someone who hasn't heard it before? What conclusions would you draw, and what teachings would you highlight?

In reflecting on the final question here, be careful to avoid drawing conclusions based merely on the moral behavior of Bible characters. That's often called moralistic interpretation, and it can be a stumbling block, distracting us from the more important message of God's work in people's lives. While we sometimes can learn from the good or bad examples portrayed by biblical heroes or villains, we do well to remember that the only person in the Bible who is righteous is God—Father, Son, and Holy Spirit. So the main character we are called to be like is God, and the main thing we are called to learn is how to live for God—that is, to love God and to love our neighbor, as Jesus explained in Matthew 22:37-40.

Lesson 5
Judges 10:6-12:15

Jephthah—from Outcast to Warrior-Leader

Introductory Notes

"Again the Israelites did evil in the eyes of the LORD" (Judg. 10:6). And so the cycle of disobedience in Israel continues.

Perhaps one of the reasons the book of Judges is in the Bible is to show how longsuffering the love of God is. By this point in the history of Israel, we might wonder why God would continue to put up with this disobedient, rebellious people. Israel keeps going back to its foolish ways in a cycle that goes from bad to worse. But God is far more patient with his people than any of us would be. For that matter, God is also greatly more patient with *us* than any of us would be.

Let's thank and praise God for his patient and longsuffering ways, and let's discover more about this God and his people in the story of Jephthah.

1. *Judges 10:6-10*
   a. The cycle of doing evil by worshiping other gods continues in Israel. Describe the depths to which the people have fallen this time.

   b. How does God respond to the people's disobedience this time?

2. *Judges 10:11-16*
   a. How eager is God to forgive this time? Explain.

b. When it comes to turning from their evil ways, the Israelites' track record is poor. Why does God show such compassion when he knows their return to him will be short-lived?

3. *Judges 10:17-11:11*
   a. What do the Israelites of Gilead (of the tribe of Manasseh) need in order to attack the Ammonites? What do they think is their best option?

   b. Give a background sketch on Jephthah. Does he seem like a reliable candidate for leading God's people? Why or why not?

   c. How does Jephthah respond to the offer by the elders of Gilead?

4. *Judges 11:12-28*
   a. Rather than simply launch an attack on the Ammonites, what does Jephthah do first?

b. What evidence does the Ammonite king offer?

c. How does Jephthah defend Israel's actions?

5. ***Judges 11:29-40***
   a. As Jephthah prepares to do battle, he makes a vow to the Lord. What is wrongheaded about this vow?

   b. When Jephthah discovers his error, what does he do?

   c. How does Jephthah's daughter react?

   d. Did Jephthah actually sacrifice his daughter?

6. *Judges 12:1-7*
   a. What do the forces of Ephraim complain about, and how does Jephthah respond?

   b. As the feud with Ephraim continues, how do the Gileadites sort out Ephraimites from their own people?

   c. Comment on the sad reality of this feuding in Israel.

7. *Judges 12:8-15*
   What do we learn about the judges cited in this section of Scripture?

Questions for Reflection

In the book of Judges we have often seen God's anger juxtaposed with his compassion. Have you ever experienced God's anger? Share an example or two, if comfortable doing so.

Conversely, in what ways have you experienced God's love and compassion?

Now, which of these can you say you've experienced more—God's anger, or God's love and compassion? Explain.

Lesson 6
Judges 13-14

Samson—Used by God in Spite of Himself

Introductory Notes

We come now to the story of Samson. Many of us have heard of this judge before—probably best known from Sunday school stories and children's videos for his superhuman strength. As adults, however, we may find that reading the whole story of Samson from the Bible gives us a few surprises. As we have learned from the stories of other judges, Samson's life reveals to us that God is indeed faithful to his purposes despite the nature of the people he works through.

1. *Judges 13:1-5*
   What happens to Manoah's wife, and what does she learn?

2. *Judges 13:6-14*
   a. What is Manoah concerned about when his wife tells him what has happened?

   b. How does the Lord respond to this concern?

3. *Judges 13:15-25*
   a. Who (or what) do Manoah and his wife think their visitor is at first?

   b. How do Manoah and his wife respond when they learn who their guest really is?

   c. What correlation do you see between Samson's being a Nazirite and the description of him in verses 24-25?

4. *Judges 14:1-4*
   a. According to Judges 13:5, Samson was set apart by God to begin "to deliver Israel from . . . the Philistines." How does his mission get off to an unlikely start?

   b. How can the writer of Judges say that "this [is] from the Lord" when Samson is deliberately disobeying God's law?

5. *Judges 14:5-14*
   a. What does Samson do when a lion attacks him? What does this tell us about him?

   b. How does Samson's gathering honey from the lion's carcass affect his Nazirite status? (See Num. 6:6-8.)

   c. Describe the process of Samson's marriage and the bet he makes at his marriage feast.

6. *Judges 14:15-20*
   a. How do the Philistines learn the answer to Samson's riddle? What does this tell us about them? About Samson's wife?

   b. After the Philistines answer Samson's riddle, how does he respond?

Questions for Reflection

What do you think of Samson as a leader during this time in the history of Israel?

Have any parts of the story reminded you of the way people act still today? If so, what does that tell you about the human condition—and, more specifically, about human sin?

Have you ever acted in some way like Samson? Like his parents? Like his wife? Like the other Philistines? Explain.

What have you learned about God in this lesson? How would you share that with someone who hasn't heard this story before?

Lesson 7
Judges 15-16

Samson—from Revenge to Ruin

Introductory Notes

The story of Samson is indeed strange. Though he is a Nazirite devoted to God, Samson disobeys God, seduces Philistine women, and takes revenge on his own account. Yet at the same time God gives Samson power against the Philistines, fulfilling the purpose of his God-appointed mission (13:5).

Samson's life story doesn't fit tidily into many of our ideas of what a leader of God's people should be. And yet God works in and through Samson to preserve his people. Scholars have noted that the Samson stories can actually *inspire* the people of God—perhaps mainly to learn that God is our strength and to serve God boldly in the brokenness of this world. While this doesn't mean we should follow Samson's behavior, it certainly can mean we should learn to trust God to use us in the work he has prepared for us (see Eph. 2:8-10).

Let's discover what happens in the rest of Samson's story—and see how God works through his life.

1. Judges 15:1-8

    a. Why won't Samson's father-in-law let Samson see his wife?

    b. How does Samson respond to this?

    c. More revenge follows; describe what takes place in verses 6-8.

2. *Judges 15:9-17*
   a. What do the Philistines decide to do next, and how does Judah react to this?

   b. How does Samson negotiate with the people of Judah?

   c. How are the Philistines surprised?

3. *Judges 15:18-20*
   How does God provide for Samson after this victory?

4. *Judges 16:1-3*
   What does Samson's visit to Gaza reveal to us?

5. *Judges 16:4-14*
   Describe the three scenes in which Samson toys with the Philistines who want to kill him.

6. *Judges 16:15-22*
   a. Why does Samson finally give in? What does he tell Delilah?

   b. What happens when the Philistines come upon Samson now?

7. *Judges 16:23-31*
   a. How do the Philistines celebrate the capture of Samson? What does this celebration reveal to us?

b. What do the Philistines do for entertainment at this celebration?

c. How does God bring defeat on the Philistines, despite their mockery and despite Samson himself?

Questions for Reflection

Some interpreters see the story of Samson as a picture of the history of Israel. Again and again they disobeyed God, drawn away by the lures of Canaanites and their gods, till they eventually met destruction. (See 2 Kings 17; 24-25; 2 Chron. 36.) Still, God worked out his purposes through this people. Reflect together on God's amazing ability to remain faithful to his people although they were rarely faithful to God.

Just because God uses imperfect people to accomplish his purposes does not mean God condones all of their behavior. Think of a time when you got off course and God gently—or not so gently—steered you back. What do you remember most about that experience?

What have you learned (or relearned) about revenge in this lesson?

If you have time, read and discuss Matthew 7:12 and its Old Testament counterpart in Leviticus 19:18. See also Romans 12:17-21 and Deuteronomy 32:35, where God says, "It is mine to avenge; I will repay." Then reflect on how God really is the one who brings judgment (as well as mercy) in this story.

Lesson 8
Judges 17-19

Rock Bottom of Moral Decay

Introductory Notes

In the remaining five chapters of Judges we are told four times that "in those days Israel had no king" (17:6; 18:1; 19:1; 21:24), and two of those statements add that "everyone did as they saw fit" (17:6; 21:24). It appears the author is looking back from the days of the monarchy in Israel to this bleak time when the religion of the day was whatever an Israelite wanted to make it. Moral decay was at an all-time low, as we will discover in this lesson.

If you haven't heard these stories before, you'll probably find them shocking. But perhaps even more shocking is that God in his mercy continues to preserve his people despite their depraved behavior.

1. **Judges 17:1-6**
   What do we learn about Micah and his mother? About the state of things in Israel?

2. **Judges 17:7-13**
   How does Micah try to manipulate God?

3. *Judges 18:1-10*
   What do the Danites need, and what do their spies recommend?

4. *Judges 18:11-26*
   a. What do the Danites do to Micah? Why?

   b. How does Micah try to retaliate? What's the result?

5. *Judges 18:27-31*
   What do the Danites do at Laish?

6. *Judges 19:1-10*
   What troubles do we discover in the households portrayed here?

7. *Judges 19:11-21*

   What kind of hospitality do the Levite and his concubine find in Gibeah?

8. *Judges 19:22-28*

   a. What troubles do the travelers face now?

   b. How does the old man compromise the hospitality he has offered?

   c. How does the Levite treat his concubine in the morning?

9. *Judges 19:29-30*

   a. What purpose could the Levite have in mind in what he does next?

40

b. How do the people of Israel react?

Question for Reflection
　Deciding that we are above the law can lead to serious misconduct. But temptations are not reserved for unbelievers. Any of us can be tempted to "do as [we] see fit." What are some steps we can take to prevent such a downward spiral?

Lesson 9
Judges 20-21

A People Divided and Still Sustained

Introductory Notes
Our Scriptures for this lesson deal with fallout from the incident of the Levite and his concubine (Judg. 19). The "wicked men" of Gibeah (19:22) have acted like the people of Sodom—or worse—and yet they are supposed to be the people of God.

How will the people of Israel deal with the Benjamites of Gibeah?

1. *Judges 20:1-7*
   a. To whom do the Israelites turn in their distress, and why?

   b. Compare the Levite's story here with the account in Judges 19:22-29. What parts of the story are different?

2. *Judges 20:8-17*
   a. What do the Israelites plan to do?

b. How does Israel try to negotiate with the Benjamites, and what is the response?

3. *Judges 20:18-25*
   a. Where do the Israelites go to seek God's help? Why? What is significant about this place?

   b. Describe the Israelites' first two rounds of battle against the Benjamites.

4. *Judges 20:26-48*
   a. How do the Israelites prepare to inquire of the Lord this time?

   b. How does God respond?

c. What is the outcome of the next battle?

5. *Judges 21:1-14*

How does Israel's oathtaking lead to a destructive decision?

6. *Judges 21:15-25*

There are still some Benjamite men without a wife. How do the Israelites propose to solve this problem?

Question for Reflection

The book of Judges paints a vivid picture of what happens when people turn their backs on God. What story or verse stands out for you as a lesson to guide your relationship with God? Why? How will you explain that to others?

An Invitation

Listen now to what God is saying to you.

You may be aware of things in your life that keep you from coming near to God. You may have thought of God as someone who is unsympathetic, angry, and punishing. You may feel as if you don't know how to pray or how to come near to God.

"But because of his great love for us, God, who is rich in mercy, made us alive with Christ even when we were dead in transgressions—it is by grace you have been saved" (Eph. 2:4-5). Jesus, God's Son, died on the cross to save us from our sins. It doesn't matter where you come from, what you've done in the past, or what your heritage is. God has been watching over you and caring for you, drawing you closer. "You also were included in Christ when you heard the word of truth, the gospel of your salvation" (Eph. 1:13).

Do you want to receive Jesus as your Savior and Lord? It's as simple as A-B-C:

- Admit that you have sinned and that you need God's forgiveness.
- Believe that God loves you and that Jesus has already paid the price for your sins.
- Commit your life to God in prayer, asking the Lord to forgive your sins, nurture you as his child, and fill you with the Holy Spirit.

Prayer of Commitment

Here is a prayer of commitment recognizing Jesus Christ as Savior. If you long to be in a loving relationship with Jesus, pray this prayer. If you have already committed your life to Jesus, use this prayer for renewal and praise.

Dear God, I come to you simply and honestly to confess that I have sinned, that sin is a part of who I am. And yet I know that you listen to sinners who are truthful before you. So I come with empty hands and heart, asking for forgiveness.

I confess that only through faith in Jesus Christ can I come to you. I confess my need for a Savior, and I thank you, Jesus, for dying on the cross to pay the price for my sins. Father, I ask that you forgive my sins and count me as righteous for Jesus' sake. Remove the guilt that accompanies my sin and bring me into your presence.

Holy Spirit of God, help me to pray, and teach me to live by your Word. Faithful God, help me to serve you faithfully. Make me more like Jesus each day, and help me to share with others the good news of your great salvation. In Jesus' name, Amen.

Bibliography

Adeyemo, Tokunboh, ed. *Africa Bible Commentary*. Grand Rapids, Mich.: Zondervan, 2006.

Auld, A. Graeme. *Joshua, Judges, and Ruth* (The Daily Study Bible Series). Louisville, Ky.: Westminster John Knox, 1984.

Barker, Kenneth L., and John R. Kohlenberger III. *Zondervan NIV Bible Commentary*. Grand Rapids, Mich.: Zondervan, 1994.

Ellison, H. L. *Scripture Union Bible Study Books: Joshua—2 Samuel*. Grand Rapids, Mich.: Eerdmans, 1966.

Elman, Yaakov. *The Living Nach: Early Prophets*. New York: Moznaim Publishing, 1994.

Elwell, Walter A., ed. *Baker Encyclopedia of the Bible*. Grand Rapids, Mich.: Baker, 1988.

Guthrie, D., and J. A. Motyer, eds. *The New Bible Commentary: Revised*. Grand Rapids, Mich.: Eerdmans, 1970.

Harris, J. Gordon, C. Brown, and M. Moore. *Joshua, Judges, Ruth* (New International Biblical Commentary). Peabody, Mass.: Hendrickson Publishers, 2000.

Keil, C. F., and F. Delitzsch. *Commentary on the Old Testament*. Grand Rapids, Mich.: Eerdmans, 1975.

Kroeger, Catherine Clark, and Mary J. Evans, eds. *The IVP Women's Bible Commentary*, Downers Grove, Ill.: InterVarsity, 2002.

Marshall, I. Howard, A. R. Millard, J. I. Packer, D. J. Wiseman, eds. *New Bible Dictionary*, Third Edition. Downers Grove, Ill.: InterVarsity, 1962.

Reardon, Patrick Henry, *Christ in His Saints*. Ben Lomond, Calif.: Conciliar Press, 2004.

TNIV Study Bible. Grand Rapids, Mich.: Zondervan, 2006.

Evaluation Questionnaire

DISCOVER JUDGES

As you complete this study, please fill out this questionnaire to help us evaluate the effectiveness of our materials. Please be candid. Thank you.

1. Was this a home group ___ or a church-based ___ program? What church?

2. Was the study used for
   ___ a community evangelism group?
   ___ a community faith-nurture group?
   ___ a church Bible study group?

3. How would you rate the materials?
   Study Guide
   ___ excellent ___ very good ___ good ___ fair ___ poor

   Leader Guide
   ___ excellent ___ very good ___ good ___ fair ___ poor

4. What were the strengths?

5. What were the weaknesses?

6. What would you suggest to improve the material?

7. In general, what was the experience of your group?

Your name (optional) _____

Address _____

_____

8. Other comments:

(Please fold, tape, stamp, and mail. Thank you.)

Faith Alive Christian Resources
2850 Kalamazoo Ave. SE
Grand Rapids, MI 49560